Do You Want to Know, Where Does a Rainbow Grow?

Written by
Kathryn Kemp Guylay

Illustrated by
Alexander Guylay

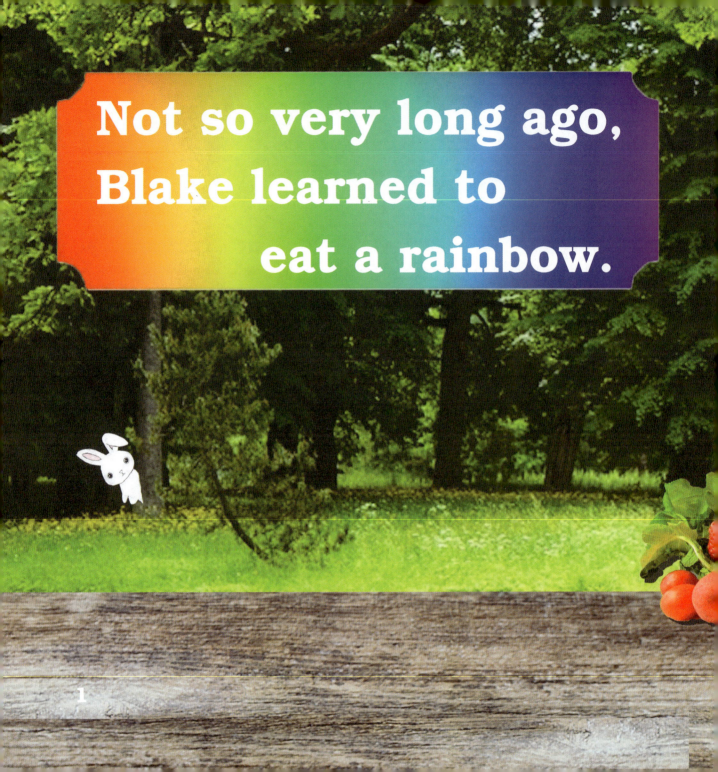

Not so very long ago, Blake learned to eat a rainbow.

A rainbow gives Blake energy and does the same for you and me!

Not all colored foods are great,

when searching for foods to fill your plate.

RED is good for the heart and mind.

RED is the first color we'll find.

 What healthy food is growing on the opposite page?

ANSWER: Tomatoes

[?] **What other RED foods are growing on the right?**

ANSWER: Cherries, strawberries, radish, red peppers

[?] **Do you want to help Blake make a rainbow basket?**

12

YELLOW and ORANGE
are good for your eyes. Look underground for a fun surprise!

 What healthy food is growing on the right?
ANSWER: Carrots

? What other YELLOW and ORANGE foods are growing on the right?

ANSWER: Peaches, pineapple, lemon, pumpkins

? After adding the lemon, how many items left until we have a rainbow in the basket?

ANSWER: Three

GREEN

- great for bones and teeth, usually does not grow underneath.

 What healthy food is growing on the right?

ANSWER: Spinach

? What other GREEN foods are growing on the right?

ANSWER: Brussels sprouts, asparagus, kiwi, broccoli

? After adding the Brussels sprouts, how many items left until we have a rainbow in the basket?

ANSWER: Two

BLUE and PURPLE

for strength overall, grow in sizes big and small.

 What healthy foods are growing on the right?

ANSWER: Eggplant, blueberries

[?] **What other BLUE and PURPLE foods are growing on the right?**

ANSWER: Kohlrabi, figs, plums, blackberries

[?] **After adding the eggplant, how many items left until we have a rainbow in the basket?**

ANSWER: Only one!

WHITE gives your tummy love. It grows underground and above.

 What healthy foods are growing on the right?

ANSWER: Cauliflower, onions

[?] **What other WHITE foods are growing to the right?**

ANSWER: Garlic, mushrooms, potatoes, turnips

[!] **You helped Blake fill a rainbow basket!**

Farmers pick food with their hands. It makes its way to produce stands.

When you eat foods from farm to table, there are very few things on the label.

About this book and the Give It a Go, Eat a Rainbow series:

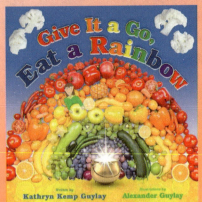

Main theme: Eating fruits and veggies is fun and gives your body energy.

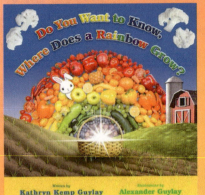

Main theme: A healthy rainbow of food comes from Mother Earth and plants.

To learn more, please visit www.giveitagoeatarainbow.com

Copyright © 2017 by Kathryn Kemp Guylay
Written by Kathryn Kemp Guylay. Learn more about Kathryn's work at www.makewellnessfun.com. Illustrated by Alexander Guylay.
Designed by Colleen Quindlen. Author photo by Christina Carlson. Images used under license from Shutterstock.com.

Published by Healthy Solutions of Sun Valley, LLC. Sun Valley, Idaho.

This book may be purchased in bulk, with special discounts, for educational, business, organizational, or promotional use. For information, please email: kg@healthysolutionsofsv.com.

All rights reserved. No part of this book may be reproduced, stored in a retrieval system, or transmitted by any means, electronic, mechanical, photocopying, recording, or otherwise, without written permission from the publisher, except for brief quotations within critical reviews or articles.
Library of Congress Control Number: 2016921429
ISBN-13: 978-0-9965328-6-0

Made in the USA
Columbia, SC
25 September 2017